EATING YOUR AUNTIE
IS WRONG

EATING YOUR AUNTIE
IS WRONG

THE WORLD'S STRANGEST CUSTOMS

 STEPHEN ARNOTT

EBURY
PRESS

3 5 7 9 10 8 6 4

Copyright © 2004 Stephen Arnott

Stephen Arnott has asserted his moral right to be identified
as the author of this work in accordance with the
Copyright, Designs and Patents Act 1988.

First published 2004 by Ebury Press,
an imprint of Random House,
20 Vauxhall Bridge Road, London SW1V 2SA

Random House Australia (Pty) Limited
20 Alfred Street, Milsons Point, Sydney, New South Wales 2061, Australia

Random House New Zealand Limited
18 Poland Road, Glenfield, Auckland 10, New Zealand

Random House South Africa (Pty) Limited
Endulini, 5a Jubilee Road, Parktown 2193, South Africa

The Random House Group Limited Reg. No. 954009

www.randomhouse.co.uk

A CIP catalogue record for this book is available from the British Library

Typesetting and cover design by seagulls

Printed and bound in Denmark by AIT Nørhaven A/S

ISBN 0 091892414

n some Aboriginal tribes slices of flesh were once taken from a corpse just before its burial. These slices were handed to the mourners to be eaten; however, certain rules governed whom could eat whom. For example, a man could eat his sister's husband and his brother's wife, but not his children. A child could not eat his or her father, while a mother was able to eat her children and vice versa.

mong the Assam of Northern India anyone who said the word 'sap' ('snake') at night immediately had to recite the names of seven bald-headed men.

n St Malo, France, fishermen poured wine down the throat of the first fish of the season they caught. The fish was then thrown back into the water. The theory was that the drunken fish would tell its friends there was free wine to be had and they'd queue up to be caught.

newly married couple in pre-Reformation England could not enjoy their wedding night until their bed had been blessed by a priest, a ceremony that traditionally took place at midnight. Some priests delayed this blessing for as long as possible in the hope they'd be bribed to speed things up

ndian parents who had produced a long line of daughters but now wanted a son would often name their last daughter 'Nati' (meaning 'no'), 'Barjii' (meaning 'prohibited'), or 'Dhapu' or 'Santosh' (both meaning 'satisfied').

irls in Lincolnshire, England, were never named 'Agnes' as it was believed that any woman with this name would eventually go insane.

n Britain it was thought lucky if a baby's first journey was upwards. For this reason a midwife would often carry a child upstairs immediately after birth. If no stairs were available the midwife might take the baby up a ladder, or jump on a stool.

he ancient Greeks thought that a woman would not conceive if she wore a cat's testicle tied in a tube across her navel.

mong the Nias people of Indonesia, if a chief was dying his job went to whoever could catch his last breath — believed to be his departing soul. The crush of claimants round a chief's deathbed could be so bad that people sometimes crawled under the hut, bored a hole through the floor, and attempted to suck out the soul using a bamboo pipe.

f a hornets' nest was found near a Sioux village, the tribe would send its young boys to visit it in the care of a warrior. The boys stripped naked and proceeded to pelt the nest with stones until it was destroyed. Any boy who cried out or showed pain as he was attacked by the furious hornets was taunted.

mong the Hottentots of South Africa a youth was initiated into manhood by being bedaubed with fat and food. The oldest man in the community then urinated over him.

n India, if a couple suffered a number of infant deaths it was assumed an evil spirit had a grudge against the family. To fool the spirit the father would take a newborn baby and give it to a neighbour or a sweeper (a profession considered lucky). Once this person had taken the child home the father would visit them and buy the baby for his 'childless' wife.

n Malaysia pregnant women were advised not to relight a fire by blowing on the embers. If they did it was thought their child would grow up to be someone who sighed frequently.

n parts of Britain it was thought that the first person to be buried in a churchyard would be carried off by the Devil. Because of this a new village graveyard was often left unused until the servant of a visitor or some other stranger happened to die in the vicinity. Sometimes a dog was killed and buried as a human substitute.

he Chinese believed that childhood sicknesses were caused by the soul escaping the body. To attract the soul back, a family member would bang on a gong to get the soul's attention, while the mother went on the roof to tempt the soul back, calling out the child's name and waving its garments on a long pole.

panish mothers used to take their children to a statue of the famous artist and architect, Mateo. The children would then have their heads banged against it in the hope it might knock some sense into them.

n India a husband whose wife was having a difficult labour might wash his big toe and give her the water to drink. The big toe was traditionally the seat of a man's strength and this was considered a way of transferring some of it to his ailing wife.

erman thieves used to try and acquire the eyeball of a dead child in the belief it would make them invisible. Conversely, a householder might try to prevent a burglary by obtaining the finger of a dead thief and burying it under his threshold.

he Malaysians thought that the corpse of a sinful man would be tortured as it lay in its grave. However, if God was merciful, the man's ghost would be released in the form of a spirit tiger which would return to protect its human family. The family kept the spirit tiger nourished on eggs. It could be asked for favours but it was considered improper to request it to eat another family member.

mong the Iroquois of North America it was thought that the first task of a dead man in the afterlife would be to sit in council with his forefathers. For this reason a corpse was placed in its grave in a sitting position.

n Mormon tradition a dead wife was laid to rest with a veil over her face. Only the husband could lift the veil and, if he did not do so, his wife would not be resurrected. According to some, the threat of not lifting the veil was often used to ensure obedience in life.

n Cheshire a pig that had given birth to a litter would be fed a bread and butter sandwich for good luck.

n Germany, wives avoided putting overly hot food on the table. According to tradition, the longer it bubbled, the longer their husbands would beat them.

mong some Britons and Scandinavians it was considered shameful for an old man to die in bed. If he felt his time was near he'd go to the nearest cliff and jump off. However, if he was too feeble to make the journey it was his son's duty to beat him to death with the family club. In the Dark Ages some churches kept a 'holy maul' for this purpose, a club that was hung on the back of the church door to be borrowed by anyone who needed it.

n many European countries it was thought to be lucky if a baby cried during its baptism as this represented the expulsion of evil from the child. If a child showed no signs of crying it was often pinched until it did.

n the Highlands of Scotland a midwife traditionally gave a newborn baby a small spoonful of earth and a tot of whisky as its first meal.

mong the Tinneh Indians of North America, it was the custom for a wife to throw herself on her husband's funeral pyre. However, she was allowed to get off again once all her hair had burnt off. She was then required to keep the pyre burning until her husband's body had been consumed, gather up his ashes, and guard them in mourning for the next two years.

n annual ceremony in ancient Greece required each householder to beat one of his slaves, then throw them out onto the streets with the words, 'Out with hunger and in with wealth and health'. This custom was also carried out at local civic buildings such as the town hall.

he Marimos of southern Africa used to sacrifice a short fat man when their crops were sown, the victim being hacked to death with hoes and rakes. It was thought that short fat men looked like the seeds they were encouraging to grow.

n the Burgundy region of France, St Urban's Day was celebrated by erecting a shrine to the saint and pouring a libation of wine over it. However, wine was only used if the weather was good — if the weather was bad it was seen as a sign of a poor harvest and the statue was pelted with dung and ditchwater.

ocal gods in China were often threatened with demotion and punishment if
they didn't do what they were told. In
1888 a statue of the god Lung-Wong was put in a
Canton prison for five days for not stopping a deluge
of rain. In a similar fashion, a statue of St Angelo
in Sicily was stripped and threatened with a hang-
ing in 1893 after failing to end a drought.

n Britain it was thought that the last person to be buried in a churchyard had to guard it until the next funeral. If two burials were scheduled for the same day there would often be a race among the mourners to get their relative buried first, thus saving them the indignity of serving as a gatekeeper.

n India a woman who wanted to make her husband obedient had to feed him a loaf of bread, the loaf being made from a quantity of flour that weighed exactly the same as her left shoe.

n the Congo it was customary to ring a bell while drinking beer. The noise was meant to scare off evil spirits that might otherwise slip down your throat with the beverage. In a similar way many west African tribes believed that your soul could escape from your mouth while you were eating, thus allowing homeless souls to invade your body. To prevent this the doors and windows of a house were firmly locked during meal times.

umatran woodcutters often tried to blame others for their tree-felling activities to avoid attacks by vengeful wood spirits. During the Colonial period one woodcutter used to read documents to the trees, claiming they were orders for a land clearance issued by the Dutch government.

n some regions of England it was customary for a husband to give his wife a cake and a large 'groaning-cheese' after she'd given birth. Sometimes the middle of the cheese was cut out and the baby passed through the hole on its christening day.

Syrian garden infested with caterpillars could be cleared if a virgin adopted one of the insects. The adopted caterpillar was buried and the virgin 'mother' went into mourning. It was hoped that the sight of the grieving girl would disturb the remaining caterpillars and make them flee. A German caterpillar remedy required the mistress of the house to walk round the garden at midnight dragging a broom. The woman had to mutter the words, 'Good evening, Mother Caterpillar — you shall come with your husband to church,' then leave the garden gate open until the morning.

armers in ancient Greece who suffered from an infestation of mice in their fields were advised to write the creatures a letter and leave it under a stone on the affected land. In the letter the farmer asked the mice to leave, suggested another field where they might go, and threatened to tear them to pieces if they didn't.

n India it was thought that if a child's nose itched it foretold the onset of a serious illness. The standard remedy was to hit the child on the nose with a shoe, then spit.

he Cham people of east Asia pretended to be drunk when gathering flax. They used to make an alcoholic drink from this plant and, in pretending to be tipsy, thought they could encourage the flax to retain its inebriating qualities.

he English considered it unlucky to pull up mandrake. If a mandrake root was required, the end of a dog's leash was tied to the plant's stem, and the dog was tempted to leap away from the plant by placing a plate of meat just out of its reach.

n Lithuania the arrival of the first new potatoes, or the first bread made from new wheat, was celebrated by everyone pulling each other's hair at the dining table.

roups of young men in Sussex and Devon used to go 'apple howling', visiting local orchards and spouting doggerel to encourage the trees to be fruitful. In return the men expected drink or money from the orchard's owner. If they didn't get it they'd return to the orchard and shout curses at the trees.

n Baganda, central Africa, the parents of twins would go to the gardens of their friends and neighbours and dance in them. In this way they hoped to pass on their fruitfulness to the vegetables.

n parts of India it was customary to give a troublesome old person a handful of supplies, put them in a large earthenware jar, and abandon them.

n Egypt the bodies of beheaded criminals were often washed on a stone slab, the dirty water and blood draining into a large stone trough that was rarely emptied. To get pregnant, barren women would pass over and under the stone table seven times, then wash their faces in the reeking, stagnant water.

any Far Eastern tribes believed that the spirit of a dead person would try to re-enter its home by the route its corpse had left it. To prevent this, a hole was made in a wall or the roof, the corpse pushed through it, and the gap quickly sealed behind.

he end of a harvest in central Europe was often marked by the ritual execution of a cock. In some areas the bird was whipped to death while in others it was bludgeoned with sticks. Some communities buried the cock up to its neck and chopped its head off with a scythe. In Transylvania the man given the job of decapitating the bird had to do it with one blow. If he didn't he was given the embarrassing nickname 'Red Cock' for the rest of the year.

apanese fruit trees were often 'encouraged' to be fruitful by threatening them with an axe.

n some Russian villages the women rolled the local priest over sprouting springtime crops to make them grow faster. If the priest objected he was reminded that, without a good harvest, he'd be going hungry.

n southern Bulgaria lumps of freshly brined cheese were thrown at newly married couples to promote fertility. Cheese was also thrown at anyone coming to the table at the St George's day feast, again to encourage health and fertility. Some farmers even brought their livestock to the feast table so they could throw cheese at their sheep.

he Lett people of the Baltic coast devoted the period between Easter and St John's Day to swinging. Every peasant spent as much of his spare time as he could swinging from a tree, believing the higher he swung, the higher his crops would grow.

ambodian protocol demanded that the king was always 'uplifted' over his subjects. To this end he never sat in a house more than one storey tall to prevent anyone walking over his head. To be doubly sure this never happened, the king's single-storey palace was given a glass roof. It was also forbidden to touch the king of Cambodia without his express permission. This custom caused problems in 1874 when the king was thrown from his carriage and knocked unconscious. None of his attendants dared touch him and it was left to a passing European to pick him up and carry him to the palace for medical attention.

n China the pillows under a dying person's head were often removed. It was thought that a person who died looking at their feet would bring misfortune on their children.

o end a dry spell Serbian villagers used to strip a girl naked then clothe her in leaves, flowers and grass. Accompanied by a choir of young women, the girl would go from house to house where each homeowner threw a bucket of water over her.

n some Indian kingdoms an ambassador who had travelled abroad was considered defiled and had to be cleansed by a rebirth. This was sometimes achieved by making the ambassador crawl through a gold model of a giant vagina. In parts of India a person who returned home after being presumed dead had to be ceremonially reborn. Part of the ceremony required the person to spend the night in an artificial womb — a barrel full of fat and water.

he duties of some west African kings were so dangerous and unpleasant that candidates had to be kidnapped and forced to take the throne.

o avoid vengeful ghosts Finnish bear hunters would try and persuade the bear's spirit that it had died by accident, for example, by being crushed under a falling tree. The bear was always given a funeral feast and its bones a decent burial. In the same way, the Nootka Indians of British Columbia dressed a dead bear in the bonnet of a chief, propped it up in a chief's tent, and offered it a meal before skinning and boiling it. The Kamtchatkans of Siberia felt guilty about killing animals for food and any creature that ended up on the dining table was always offered food itself. In this way it was hoped the animal would consider itself an honoured guest and not just the main course. It was also thought the animal's spirit would communicate with its living relatives and encourage them to get caught, so they too could enjoy a good meal.

n India a newborn baby who would not suckle might be punished by being placed in a linen hammock and suspended in the branches of a tree. If the baby still refused to suckle after the third day it was assumed to be a devil and thrown into the Ganges.

hile they were away, east African elephant hunters had their wives watched to make sure they were faithful. If a wife committed adultery it was thought that an elephant would acquire power over her husband and kill him. In the same way, the Moxos Indians of Bolivia believed that if a wife were unfaithful a snake would bite her husband. The wives of men who suffered snakebites were often executed on the spot.

o cure a headache the ancient Egyptians used to inhale the smoke from burning sandals.

n North America the Algonquins and Huron Indians used to marry their fishing nets to young girls. It was thought the nets would be happier with wives and more likely to catch fish.

he Inuit of the Bering Straits kept the bladders of every animal they killed. They believed an animal's soul resided in its bladder and, during an annual ceremony, the tribe's bladder collection was pushed through a hole in the ice so the animals could be reborn and hunted again.

he Romans believed that cutting your hair at sea would bring bad luck. The belief survived in the Royal Navy and British sailors only had their hair cut during a violent storm, the logic being that the weather could not possibly get any worse.

very year the people of Abonsam, a town on the west coast of Africa, used to scare away evil spirits by screaming loudly, firing muskets, beating pans, and throwing lighted torches. To make these tactics more effective the event was preceded by four weeks of utter silence.

n India a single sneeze was considered bad luck, but multiple sneezing was good. Someone sneezing to your front or right meant bad luck, while sneezes from the rear or left were good. If someone sneezed while sowing seeds, applying medicine, or starting an education it was a sign of sure success. The sneeze of a quadruped, a person standing at a window, a man with dishevelled hair, or someone carrying torture instruments was always very bad luck.

mong the Greeks it was thought that small goblins called Kalikatzaroi invaded the house on Christmas Day. House fires were kept going to stop them coming down the chimney and old shoes were burnt to create an unpleasant smell.

n Madagascar it was thought that anyone born on the first day of February would have their hut burn down later in life. To cheat this fate, infants born on this day were placed in a hut that was deliberately burnt down around them, the children only being rescued at the last minute.

ndians living in the Amazon delta believed that a man's penis size could be increased using the fruit of an aquatic plant called 'aninga'. The aninga fruit resembles a banana and it was used to thrash the man's genitals soundly for three days before a full moon.

he ancient Romans believed you could stop yourself having unpleasant thoughts by wetting a finger with spit and rubbing it behind your ear.

n some Aboriginal tribes of New South Wales it was believed that men who had any contact with their mothers-in-law would suffer terrible luck. The threat was so great that married men even avoided looking in their mother-in-law's general direction.

n Sierra Leone an elected king was beaten with sticks on his coronation. Unfortunately some kings were beaten so hard they died. Unpopular men were sometimes elected king simply so they could be disposed of. In the Ngoi province of Congo it was customary to kill the king on the night after his coronation. Not surprisingly the throne was always vacant.

lavic shoplifters used to burn blind cats to death and throw a pinch of their ash over unsuspecting shopkeepers. It was believed this would prevent the shopkeeper noticing their pilfering.

n India a sorcerer could injure an enemy by muttering the Arabic spell 'Ya khe ha ro' 10,000 times a day for 21 days. The name of the enemy was then written on an unbaked brick and three spells uttered; the first one a single time, the second 41 times, and the last 1000 times. After every ten repetitions the brick would be hit with a shoe, the victim supposedly feeling every blow.

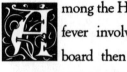mong the Hausa of west Africa a cure for fever involved writing a prayer on a board then washing the ink off with water and drinking it. A similar cure for hiccups required you to write down the names of seven liars.

n seventeenth-century England it was thought that a pregnant woman who ate beans and onions would give birth to a lunatic. These foods were thought to poison a baby's brain with noxious vapours.

mong the Moors one headache cure required you to select a lamb or a goat then beat it until it fell over. This treatment was thought to transfer the pain from the man to the beast.

n India it was customary for two people who'd banged heads together accidentally to bang them together a second time. If not, it was thought that bad luck would follow.

he Karen people of Myanmar believed a corpse could suck out the souls of the young. If a funeral procession passed near a house the children inside would be secured with special strings to prevent their souls being dragged from them.

he Hungarians believed that a barren woman could be cured of her infertility by her being beaten with a stick, the stick having previously been used to separate a pair of mating dogs.

mong the Javanese the soul was believed to be bird-shaped and could be knocked free if someone hit his or her head badly. If a man suffered such an injury his wife would visit the scene of the accident and scatter grain while making clucking sounds to attract the soul-bird. The grain was then picked up and sprinkled over the husband's head to encourage the soul-bird to return.

mong the Mbaya Indians of South America, parents killed every child born to them except the one they believed would be their last. Any other children born subsequently were also killed. Not surprisingly this custom caused some branches of the tribe to die out altogether.

Slavic love charm required a girl to dig up the footprint of the man she loved, put the soil in a plant-pot, and use it to plant a marigold. It was believed that a marigold never faded and, in the same way, the man's love would last forever.

n England, clay from a parson's grave was thought to be good for curing a variety of ailments. It was taken internally after being boiled into a soup.

n India it was considered polite to clap your hands three times if you were caught short and had to defecate in a field. The clapping was designed to warn the local spirits so they could leave the vicinity.

n parts of Russia it was thought that a drought could be ended by stripping an old woman, tying her to a plough, and driving her through the village at midnight. Another Russian drought remedy was to find the corpse of a man who had died of drink, dig him up and throw him in a lake. In southern Russia it was thought rain could be encouraged if the women of the village grabbed hold of a passing stranger and threw him in a river. In Armenia the same was done to the wife of the local priest.

n many parts of the world it was believed that if a bird found a strand of your hair and used it to build a nest, you would suffer from headaches.

any tribes in central Australia kept a large bank of dried human foreskins. The foreskins were thought to have magical rainmaking properties.

n Lapland it was the custom for a young man out courting to keep his prospective father-in-law supplied with regular gifts of brandy. To maintain this supply, fathers traditionally delayed the marriage of their daughters for as long as possible.

n some regions of India, mango trees had to be married before their fruit could be eaten. Mango trees were traditionally wedded to tamarind or jasmine trees.

mong the Arabs, widows were thought to be extremely unlucky. At the wedding of a widow no one would eat any bread, and no one would use their hostess' eating utensils, bringing their own cups and plates instead. The widow's new husband would do likewise and refuse to eat her food or use anything she'd touched until a month after the wedding.

hinese brides used to suffer a three-day ceremony called 'nao-sin-fang'. During this time any person might demand to see the bride and insult her with impertinent and ribald remarks.

n seventeenth-century England it was thought that a case of measles could be cured by laying a live sheep on the bed of the patient.

ccording to the Masai of east Africa, children who played with their lamp shadows would wet the bed.

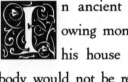n ancient Athens if someone died owing money, his debtors could enter his house and seize his corpse. The body would not be released for burial until the debt had been paid.

arriageable girls in ancient Assyria were regarded as the property of the state and sold at public market. The money collected filled the government coffers but, to help ensure that even the ugly girls found husbands, some money was set aside as 'cashback' for any man who bid for one of the unattractive ones.

n India members of the Bonthuk caste would add a bound pig to the orchestra playing at a wedding. It was thought that the squeals of the pig, added to the noise of instruments, would help frighten evil spirits away from the bride and groom.

n the Middle Ages a German bride-groom stamped on his bride's toes to signify his dominance over her. These days the bride and groom compete to see who can stand on the other's feet.

n many parts of Europe it was thought very lucky if a fisherman and his wife argued before he went out for the day. If the couple came to blows and the man drew blood he'd have an exceptionally good catch. In Scotland it was considered very bad luck to wish a fisherman good luck. If you did so, he could only cancel the ill effect by punching you until he drew blood.

n English Easter tradition involved women beating their husbands on Easter Tuesday, and their husbands beating their wives on Easter Wednesday. The custom was last recorded taking place in the city of Durham.

Persian gentleman was expected to marry a woman of equal social stature. However, if a man wanted to form an attachment with a woman from a lower social order he was allowed to hire her on a 99-year lease.

mong the Tartars, the relations of the bride and bridegroom would divide into two groups and fight each other until someone had suffered bleeding wounds. It was thought that causing blood to flow in this way ensured the couple would have strong sons.

n the German town of Munchen-Gladbach, 'Women's Day' was celebrated in mid-February. The local women disguised themselves as crones, took over the town hall, then went singing and dancing in the streets, where they cut off the tie of any man who fell into their clutches.

he farmers of East Anglia used to test the readiness of the soil for seed-sowing by taking off their trousers and sitting bare-bottomed on the ground.

mong the Tinneh people of North America girls did not have their finger-nails cut until they were four years old. It was thought that cutting them any earlier would make the girls lazy.

he ancient Romans thought it bad luck for a person to enter a house with their left foot. Some households employed a slave whose only duty was to prevent the home being entered left-foot-forward.

n rural England it was thought that a rain storm could be stopped by making the eldest child of the house strip naked, go outside and stand on their head.

ccording to German tradition the use of bad language would lead to a dramatic increase in the local mouse population.

ustom forbade Mongols from dipping their hands into water. To clean their hands they'd take a mouthful of water, spit it out in a long stream, and wash in that.

n Turkey it was thought that passing soap to someone would lead to an argument. To avoid this, you proffered soap to another person on the back of your hand.

mong the Marvas of India an arranged marriage had to go ahead even if the bride or bridegroom died before the ceremony. The living partner was married to the corpse but free to find a living partner immediately afterwards.

n sixteenth-century Europe, eating raw cat meat was considered a cure for asthma. An alternative was to drink the foam from a mule's mouth.

mong the Korku tribe of India, a father would capture a marriage partner for his daughter and make the young man serve as a household slave for up to a year. If the boy seemed suitable he then had a year to make the girl pregnant. If he failed he was chased out of the house.

An old German love charm required a girl to procure a shoe belonging to her beloved, and urinate in it.

I n Portugal it was thought a husband could ease the labour pains of his wife by lifting and turning a tile taken from a church roof.

European cure for constipation was to eat bacon. However, to be effective the bacon had to be stolen.

n rural England and the backwoods of America it was said that a child could be cured of whooping cough if it rode on the back of a bear. Another English whooping cough cure was to eat bread and butter provided by a married couple named John and Joan.

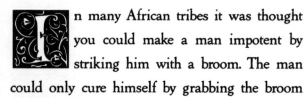n many African tribes it was thought you could make a man impotent by striking him with a broom. The man could only cure himself by grabbing the broom and thrashing you with it.

he people of Kelso, Scotland, used to place a cat in a barrel of soot and hang it between two tall poles. Men would then ride under the barrel and hit it with clubs and mallets. The object of the sport was to smash the barrel without an angry sooty cat landing on your head.

In northern India a man who'd lost more than two wives would try to shake off his bad luck by marrying a sheep or a plant.

Cornish cure for thrush involved fasting for three consecutive days then having your mouth blown into by a posthumous child, meaning one whose father had died before it was born.

n seventeenth-century Newcastle habitual drunks were made to wear a beer barrel with holes cut out for their arms. They were then paraded through the streets.

n some North American tribes, a death in the community meant everyone had to change their name. It was believed that all the people in the village were listed to die in a certain order. However, when Death returned it would be confused by the mass renaming, think it had come to the wrong place and go away.

report of 1797 described a ceremony called the Crab Wake held in the village of St Kenelm in Shropshire. Apparently this tradition involved the locals getting together to throw crabs at each other.

n Mexico it was thought that anyone watching an animal defecate would develop a stye in his or her eye.

ad luck at sea was often attributed to the presence of a 'Jonah'. On a Scottish ship, if the identity of the Jonah was not obvious, the ship's cook might bake a piece of wood or a nail into a loaf of bread. Whoever bit into the nail or wood at dinner time was the unlucky one and would be thrown off the ship.

n rural America it was thought that a girl wanting a new dress could charm herself one by catching a butterfly. Once caught, the girl mashed the butterfly between her teeth in the hope she'd get a dress in the same colour.

he Masai of east Africa believed that anyone who ate straight from the cooking pot would have heavy rain on their wedding day.

n England a single white hair removed from an otherwise black cat was considered a good luck charm. However, to be effective you had to pull the hair out without being scratched or bitten.

central European cure for baldness required the sufferer to eat some pubic hairs mixed into a fresh bowl of chicken soup.

ccording to Islamic tradition a housefly carried poison on one of its wings and an antidote on the other. If a fly fell in your soup you were advised to duck the fly under the surface before removing it. This ensured the poison and antidote would cancel each other out.

n Germany it was thought that a rainy morning could be turned into a sunny afternoon if all the old women in the vicinity cleared their throats.

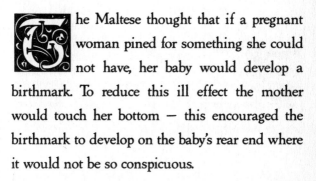

he Maltese thought that if a pregnant woman pined for something she could not have, her baby would develop a birthmark. To reduce this ill effect the mother would touch her bottom — this encouraged the birthmark to develop on the baby's rear end where it would not be so conspicuous.

n China a small boy (preferably born in a Dragon year) was rolled across the matrimonial bed of newly-weds to ensure their fertility.

n northern Europe a woman wishing to know the identity of her future husband ate salted herring before going to bed. Her husband would then appear in a dream bringing her a refreshing glass of water.

ome tribes of ancient Peru ground the bones of deceased relatives and mixed them with fermented liquor. This concoction was then drunk, the reasoning being that the remains would be better off inside a loved one than in a hole in the ground. In a similar fashion, members of certain Tibetan tribes made drinking cups out of the skulls of their parents so they could join in with the fun at festivals.

The Dutch considered it unwise to carry on private conversations in the presence of a cat. It was thought that cats had a magical ability to spread gossip.

n pre-Columbian Mexico being drunk was a privilege of men over the age of 70. If a younger man was found drunk his head was shaved and his house destroyed. If he was found drunk a second time he was killed. A man who died due to an excess of drink was often eaten.

n Northern Ireland a man eating eggs had to consume an even number — if not it was thought his horses would succumb to mischief. Another belief meant you could not praise a horse without spitting on it afterwards. If a horse fell sick after being praised, the owner had three days to find the person who'd paid the compliment and get them to say the Lord's Prayer in the horse's ear.

n parts of the Congo a man caught committing adultery had to give the woman's husband a slave as compensation. If he could not do so, he became a slave himself. This compensation scheme could be very lucrative, resulting in some men deliberately using their attractive wives as lures.

baby boy in Fiji was encouraged to strike his mother as soon as he was capable. If not it was feared he would grow up to be a coward.

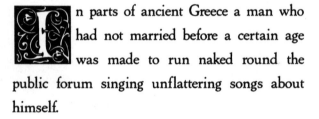 n parts of ancient Greece a man who had not married before a certain age was made to run naked round the public forum singing unflattering songs about himself.

n France it was thought that bouts of vomiting were caused by an 'unhooked stomach'. To effect a cure, men could be hired who threw themselves on the floor in front of the patient, pretended to unhook their own stomachs, then went through the motions of hooking them up again. It was thought the sufferer's stomach would follow the example and reattach itself.

n Java it was customary for women to put out house fires. The men were kept busy forming a cordon round the burning property to prevent thieves making off with valuables.

he Inuit of Greenland used to play a game where they hammered each other on the back with clenched fists. The one who could stand up to the longest hammering was the winner.

n the Marianne Islands a woman who discovered her husband was having an affair would put on her husband's hat and summon all her female friends. Armed with sticks they went to the husband's fields to tear up his crops, then broke up his property and beat him up. On the other hand, if the woman had an affair, all her husband could do was ask for a separation.

A mong the Algonquin Indians a dog was considered man's most faithful and valuable companion. If a man was entertaining an honoured guest, the host could pay his visitor the highest compliment by killing his dog and serving it up for dinner.

n ancient Athens, if a man was unable to give his wife children she was entitled to rope in his nearest male relation as a substitute bed-partner.

mong the Persians butting the ends of eggs against each other was a popular pastime. Players were very competitive and a particularly strong egg was considered a valuable asset.

n Peru it was customary to close your mouth and put a hand over your face if you saw a rainbow. If not it was thought your teeth would rot.

n parts of the Philippines a man wishing to visit his fiancée had to pay to enter her house. He also had to pay to speak with her, and pay again to eat with her. The money spent in this way was pocketed by his future in-laws.

he Poles considered it unlucky to refuse the request of a pregnant woman. If you did, mice would come and chew your clothes.

n Bulgaria it was thought that a woman should only be completely clean once in her life. This occasion was the ceremonial bath a bride took on the night before her wedding. Meanwhile, in the English Midlands it was thought that a girl who got married wearing no underwear would be lucky in later life.

mong the Kamschatdale people of Russia, a marriage ceremony started with the bridegroom trying to strip the bride naked. The bride was prepared for this and — strapped into her clothes — she fought off the bridegroom with the help of her women friends. Eventually the scratched and bitten suitor would be forced to give up. The ceremony only continued if the bride begged the bridegroom to try again.

n many parts of the world it's thought that if three people are photographed together one will soon die — usually the one in the middle.

mong the Mingrelians of the Caucasus, married women often took lovers. A husband was not expected to complain in these circumstances as the more lovers his wife had the more valued she was. Arguments between married couples were usually settled by the local chief who solved the problem by selling one of the pair as a slave.

he Koreans considered it a grave offence to write someone's name in red ink. It meant you wanted them to die.

n parts of Europe it was thought that cutting bread unevenly was a sign that you had been telling lies.

n many places a mixture of sun and rain was considered bad luck. The Maltese used to say that 'a Turk has been born' if the sun shone while it rained. In Germany it was believed that poison fell from the sky when it rained in sunshine.

On his death, the king of Abeokuta, west Africa, was beheaded and his head put in an earthenware jar. The jar was then presented to the new king whose first official act was to eat the tongue of the old one.

n the Philippines anyone getting a bump on the head would immediately have their chin slapped upwards. This was thought to knock their brain back into place.

n China the clothes a person was to be buried in were usually made years in advance and elderly people often took their 'grave clothes' out of storage to wear on their birthdays. Young girls made these garments as it was thought their youthful vitality would become impregnated in the fabric and help postpone death.

n many parts of Greece it was considered unlucky to receive a compliment. If you got one you had to say the word 'garlic' and spit on yourself three times. If you knew the person who gave the compliment, you could ask them to spit on you as well.

n Ireland, if a mother or father thought their baby was a fairy changeling they hid a set of bagpipes under its cot. If the child was a fairy it would be unable to resist the temptation of playing them.

he Turks thought that any man who happened to walk between two girls would thereafter only be able to grow a very sparse beard.

n Hyderabad, India, a bride traditionally ran away from the bridal pavilion and was chased by the priest. While the priest dragged her back, the girl's relatives pelted him with rice, betel nuts and tamarinds. It was considered very good luck if the priest was injured or cried out as a result.

he Romanians believed you could ward off curses by wearing your underwear inside out.

n parts of the Congo a man's death was usually accompanied by a large funeral party. At the party the man's widow had to have sex with anyone who asked her, the only condition being that the act was carried out in private and in complete silence.

SELECT REFERENCES

Ashley, Leonard (1986) *The Wonderful World of Superstition, Prophecy and Luck*. New York: Dembner Books.

Baudesson, Henry (1919) *Indo-China and its Primitive People*. London: Hutchinson.

Doré, Henry (1987) *Chinese Customs*. Singapore: Graham Brash.

Drazheva, Raina (1982) *Bulgarian Folk Customs and Rituals*. Sofia: Septemvri Publishing House.

Dubois, Abbé J.A. (1999) *Hindu Manners, Customs and Ceremonies*. Delhi: Book Faith India.

Frazer, Sir James George (1994) *The Golden Bough: A Study in Magic and Religion, Magical Beliefs and Superstitions*, London: Oxford University Press.

Khanna, Dr Girija and Khanna, Hari Mohan (1974) *All About Superstitions*. Delhi: Vikas Publishing House.

Lambert, l'Abbé (c. 1750) *Curious Observations Upon the*

Manners, Customs, Languages, Religion, Natural History, Commerce, Arts, and Sciences of the Several Nations of Asia, Africa and America. London.

Lewis, Don (1972) *Curious and Humorous Customs.* Oxford: Mowbray.

Mohtar, Haji (1979) *Malay Superstitions and Beliefs.* Kuala Lumpur: Federal Publications.

Pegg, Bob (1981) *Rites and Riots: Folk Customs of Britain and Europe.* Poole: Blandford Press.

Rajkhowa, Benudhar (1973) *Assamese Popular Superstitions and Assamese Demonology.* Gauhati: Dept. of Folklore Research, Gauhati University.

Scott, George Ryley (1953) *Curious Customs of Sex and Marriage.* London: Torchstream Books.

Strong, James C. (1893) *Wah-Kee-Nah and Her People. The Curious Customs, Traditions, and Legends of the North American Indians.* New York: G.P. Putnam's Sons.

Tremearne, Major A. (1913) *Hausa Customs and Superstitions.* London: John Bale.

Waring, Philippa (1997) *Dictionary of Omens and Superstitions.* London: Souvenir Press.